Wisdom from
the Batcave

Also by Cary Friedman

Table for Two
Marital Intimacy
Spiritual Survival for Law Enforcement

Wisdom from the Batcave

How to Live a Super, Heroic Life

CARY A. FRIEDMAN

compass
books

Wisdom from the Batcave
How to Live a Super, Heroic Life
by Cary A. Friedman

Published by:
Compass Books
"Books that point the way"
P.O. Box 3091
Linden, NJ 07036
batwisdom.com

Interior design by Alan Barnett, Inc.

Printed in the United States of America

Library of Congress Cataloging-in-Publication Data
Friedman, Cary A.
Wisdom from the Batcave
How to Live a Super, Heroic Life
p. cm.
Includes bibliographical references (p.).
ISBN: 978-0-9761966-2-4
1. Spirituality 2. Pop culture / comic books
3. Psychology / Self-help
Library of Congress Control Number: 2006905272

Imperial Impressions, Inc.

Printing and binding by Imperial Impressions, Inc.
473 Sylvan Avenue, Englewood Cliffs, NJ 07632
www.imperialimpressions.biz
Phone: (201) 960-1804

For my brother, Barry

In memoriam Thomas and Martha Wayne

In memoriam Bob Kane and Bill Finger,
the fathers of the Batman

Dedicated to the many talented men
and women who have faithfully
chronicled the adventures of the
Batman for close to 70 years

Dedicated to Raoul Wallenberg, Giorgio Perlasca,
Oskar Schindler, Aristides de Sousa Mendes,
Chiune and Yukiko Sugihara

ACKNOWLEDGEMENTS

A special thank you to Grandmaster Richard Ailes [Si Tai Gung], Greg Aker [Fu Chuan] and William B. Kushnick [Chien Tao] of the Ailes School of Gung Fu. They are worthy mentors in the finest sense of the word.

Denny O'Neil and Jordan Gorfinkel have been supportive throughout the writing of this book. I am proud to consider them my friends.

I am grateful to Shani Sipzner Benedict, Yanki Brachfeld, Shmulie Brown, Harry Elias, Moshie Krohn, Pete Mandle, Lisa Mulman, and Eric Shoag for their critical contributions to the book and its author.

Efrem Zimbalist, Jr. is every bit as gracious and noble as the heroes he has portrayed over the years. I am grateful to Mr. Zimbalist for his keen review of the manuscript and his beautiful comments that grace this volume.

It is a pleasure to work with talented professionals like Adam Simms and Alan Barnett. Adam is a first-rate editor and Alan is a top-notch graphic artist. I thank them for their invaluable assistance in producing a beautiful, accurate volume.

My wife Marsha is, for me, the living embodiment of the lessons I describe in this book. The only reason she did not write it herself is that the people who are busy living their lives in accordance with these principles rarely have the time to write books about them. Without her encouragement, patience, wisdom, love, and editorial expertise, neither this book nor anything else I have ever done would exist.

Praise for
Wisdom from the Batcave

It was a rough neighborhood I grew up in back in Philadelphia. And a kid needed some guidelines to make sure he didn't follow the wrong path. The nuns at St. Andrews would have been horrified to learn that sometimes What Would Batman Do was of more practical use than anything contained in my Catechism. Bruce Wayne, and the man he would become, spoke to me more than the other costumed do-gooders I read about because he wasn't transformed by a lightning bolt, magic ring or the benefit of extraterrestrial origin. He became the Dark Knight Detective through dedication and courage and hard work. That meant that if I stayed in school, obeyed my parents and ate my vegetables then I could be a hero. That's the message that seeped into my brain from the thousands of pages of comic books that I read and re-read throughout my childhood.

Rabbi Friedman beautifully articulates the lessons and meaning and source of inspiration that Batman provided for me and millions of other kids; what we assimilated as kids through countless hours of following the struggles and solving the mysteries and going into combat beside Batman and Robin. The Rabbi distills that experience elegantly and provides a lesson even for the already-initiated. This book makes the case better than anything that I have ever read for why Bob Kane's creation continues to fascinate (and instruct) decades after his first appearance.

—Chuck Dixon
Writer, *Batman, Nightwing, Robin, Birds of Prey, Batgirl,* and *Catwoman*

Cary Friedman understands Batman in the largest possible sense: as a character, as entertainment, as modern mythology and as an exemplar of moral and ethical values. His book is the best of its kind I've ever read and I've given copies of it to the writers and artists who produce our stories with the promise that they'll both enjoy it and learn from it.

—Dennis O'Neil
Group Editor, Retired
Batman Comics

It was with a bemused skepticism that I sat down to read *Wisdom from the Batcave*. The idea of equating man's highest and noblest aspirations with a cartoon character seemed outrageous, to put it mildly.

I couldn't have been more mistaken. With his brilliant analysis and fearless postulations, Rabbi Friedman has shown why, in an era of timidity, correctness and lassitude, Batman, by his own code of honor, is able to leapfrog over the demons that cause police, armies, and nations to pause.

A spectacular book!

—Efrem Zimbalist, Jr.

The greatest heroes of literature are inspirational not because of their feats and powers but because of their ethics and their integrity. The dream of stopping bank robbers and super-villains like Batman does isn't something we can realistically aspire to—but each and every one of us can find within us a path to personal heroism, and Cary Friedman provides the roadmap. This is one terrific read.

—Mark Waid
Writer, *Justice League of America*

When Bruce Wayne was a child, his parents were gunned down in a random street crime. In response, he swore to spend his life warring on criminals. In the black and white world of comics, he could easily have become a black and white caricature—but something wonderful happened. He inspired his writers over the years to find the nobility in themselves and personify it through him; the Batman became a man who faces darkness but sees in shades of gray. He lives every moment on the edge of greatness because that's his very human choice. That's the kernel of the wisdom that Rabbi Friedman has uncovered in the Batcave. If you wouldn't be caught dead reading a comic book, be caught alive reading this book, and see what the Batman inspires in you.

—Steve Englehart
Writer, *Batman, Justice League
of America, Avengers,* and *Fantastic Four*

Wisdom from the Batcave is a thoughtful exploration of the moral messages one can discover in the Batman mythology. Cary has done a wonderful job analyzing comicdom's most complex creation, and, in the process, shown that there is a Batman inside all of us.

—Gerry Conway
Co-Executive Producer,
Law & Order Criminal Intent

People will never know what changes the direction of their lives. For Bruce Wayne, it was the murder of his parents. For many who read Batman's adventures, they have chosen to become protectors and helpers. Those subtle lessons contained in the four-color adventures are carefully explored in this labor of love. As the Rabbi has changed aspects of his life as a result of these studies, we can only hope that readers will be equally inspired to improve their lives and, through their actions, create a better world.

—Robert Greenberger
Former DC Comics Editor

Wisdom from the Batcave is not only a love letter to comics, but also a touching celebration of life's most basic treasures and humanity's ongoing quest for nobility, greatness, and integrity, as observed through the Batman's cowl.

With an earnest, conversational style, Cary Friedman reminds us what it feels like to enter the mysterious depths of the Batcave for the first time as a wide-eyed child, and illustrates how we can carry with us the artifacts found therein to the real, complicated, often troubling world.

Charming, spiritual, and inspirational, *Wisdom* unabashedly embraces the fantasies of the Batman mythology, and translates them into simple earnest truths for the everyday superhero.

— Joe Kelly

Why has the Caped Crusader endured so long as a paradigm of heroism in our collective consciousness? With his insightful deconstruction of the Dark Knight, Cary Friedman provides the answer by illustrating that above all else the most important item in Batman's utility belt is a moral compass. Rabbi Friedman realizes that Bruce Wayne's purpose-driven existence can also be a primer for any troubled soul to walk in the shadow of the Batman when facing the adversity and adversaries of this world.

—Scott Beatty
Author, *Batman: The Ultimate Guide to the Dark Knight* and *The Batman Handbook*

I thought I knew Batman, from years of writing him. I thought I understood how Batman and the real world related to each other. What I didn't know was how much Batman and his code had affected me, until I read this book. A fascinating read, and a real eye-opener.

—Ed Brubaker
Writer of *Batman, Catwoman, Daredevil,* and *Gotham Central*

When I was a kid and started to read comic books, I never tried to analyze them or ponder the good and evil of characters or story content. I only enjoyed them (as I do to this day) and thrilled to the effect they had on my imagination. It was the time of the birth of comic books and they determined my future as a cartoonist.

Now, Rabbi Friedman has given reason and understanding to my motivation and commitment. The book he has written is a source of inspiration for all, regardless of the road we choose to travel.

— Joe Kubert

In the 1950s much was made about the so-called immorality of comic books, but in fact, with rare exceptions, comics have always taught moral lessons—some obvious, some subtle. *Wisdom from the Batcave* perceptively shines a light on both kinds as manifested in the Batman mythos—an excellent book not just for fans of the Batman, but one to be given to anyone who doubts that there is morality, value, and yes, wisdom, in graphic storytelling.

—Alan Brennert
Novelist, Screenwriter,
Batman Writer

I started reading super-hero comic books at the dawn of the Silver Age when I was about eight years old. I have often attributed much of my personal philosophy to the ideals set by Superman. But after reading Cary Friedman's *Wisdom from the Batcave*, I realized how much I owe to Batman as well. If there was any need for proof that fictional characters can be as influential to our lives as real people, this book provides it.

—Bob Rozakis
Former DC Production
Director and Writer

Cary Friedman's *Wisdom from the Batcave* is entertaining and inspirational. Drawing upon the entire Bat Cave-sized oeuvre, Friedman finds a path to follow in Bruce Wayne's heroic reaction to the tragedy of his parents' deaths and applies these lessons to everyday life. The book skips through Bats' history with numerous illustrations that will have aficionados digging for their back-issues. An excellent addition to anyone's library.

—Mike Baron
Co-creator of Nexus and Badger

Bat fans and general readers alike will find much wisdom in this refreshing take on the underlying lessons of this great popular culture hero.

—Max Allan Collins,
creator of *Road to Perdition*

When young Bruce Wayne suffered the worst loss imaginable, he stood vulnerable and traumatized at the precipice of momentous choice. In his never-fading pain, he nevertheless chose compassion over hatred. Justice, not revenge. He chose to counter everything inflicted upon him, doing his utmost to prevent the same violent tragedy from befalling others.

Indeed, Bruce Wayne chose to remake himself as the Batman, a figure merely cloaked in darkness, his soul compelled by the forces of a light never dimmed.

And from this choice, so utterly simple yet ultimately profound, all things positive flowed: Courage, heroism, loyalty, trust, empathy, and the indomitable strength of selfless decency.

Rabbi Cary Friedman's wise and absorbing book sheds light on the seeming paradox of Bruce Wayne's choice, penetrating the cloak of darkness to reveal the Batman's inner truth.

—Doug Moench
Writer, *Batman, Master of
Kung Fu, Moon Knight*

To me, the Batman is not a fantasy, but a guidebook of what I might strive to be, a measure by which I may gauge myself.

The world around us has lessons about what we can aspire to achieve, and you don't have to look very far to find those lessons. These values can be found in the best comic books, and the very best comic book character is one who has no super-powers at all and whose achievements are a direct result of his values!

That's the secret of the Batman and the lesson of Cary Friedman's *Wisdom from the Batcave*. At their best, comic books are about our highest aspirations, about sacrifice, love, trust, kindness, brotherhood, and, above all, being prepared. And, as it turns out (and we always knew) in comics, Batman is the spokesperson for these values.

—Neal Adams

After a lifetime of reading, writing and, yes, studying comic books, I didn't think there were many angles I'd left unconsidered in my understanding of the form, but Rabbi Friedman has taken the hyper-muscular realm of the fantastic and found in it everyday, commonsense lessons for living a richer, fuller life. Superheroes leap tall buildings in a single bound; *Wisdom from the Batcave* provides the rest of us with a roadmap for accomplishing the equally heroic, and perhaps more difficult, task of leading a good life.

—Paul Kupperberg,
writer and former Editor,
DC Comics

There is no shortage of writings about comics in general, or Batman in particular. Yet Cary Friedman has managed to produce a book which is absolutely unique in its approach. What's even better is that it's simply one of the finest and most thought-provoking—an outstanding contribution to this field.

—Scott Peterson
Writer, *The Gotham Adventures*

Rabbi Friedman's work on the spirituality inherent in the best parts of the nearly 70 years of Batman mythos reveals not only why that character has endured in popularity for so long, but why he deserves to. One part of his book that particularly struck home with me is the eternal tension in our lives between "law" and "justice." So often when I pick up a newspaper or watch TV news, I've felt mentally torn 'twixt the difference between those two ideals, which ought to be identical but which, of course, so often are not. The four-color career of Batman holds up a mirror to life and invites us—nay, dares us—to work out for ourselves which of the two to value more highly.

—Roy Thomas
Writer, *Conan the Barbarian,*
The Avengers, The X-men, All-Star Squadron
Retired Editor-in-chief, Marvel Comics
Editor, *ALTER EGO*

Beyond providing significant inspirational value, *Wisdom from the Batcave* unveils the human element that has turned an important popular culture icon from an enduring hero of graphic prose into a fount of inspiration for millions of readers. This book is a worthy and necessary tool for understanding the American culture.

—Mike Gold
President and Editorial Director,
ComicMix LLC

In *Wisdom from the Batcave,* Cary Friedman reveals the Light in the Dark Knight. While I discuss Batman only briefly in my book on Superman, *The Gospel According to the Worlds Greatest Superhero,* Friedman makes me wish I'd dealt with Bats more. The truths he exposes about why the Caped Crusader appeals to us are timely, insightful, and important. It's an essential read for any Batman fan.

—Stephen Skelton
Author, *The Gospel According to*
the World's Greatest Superhero

CONTENTS

Wisdom from
the Batcave

FOREWORD

What a crazy, eventful history this book has already had, even before it has hit the bookstores! The story I'm about to tell you is completely true, but I'll understand if you don't quite believe it. Even though I have lived it, I sometimes have a hard time believing it myself.

I wrote the basic manuscript for *Wisdom from the Batcave* in 1999, while I was a chaplain at Duke University. I wrote it because of my love for the Batman (and what he represents) and my desire to help regular people— starting with myself—translate his heroic ideals into their everyday lives.

What I didn't expect—didn't even dream!—was that soon, because of "the Batman book" (as I called it), I would be working as a consultant to the FBI. But that's what happened. Since Spring 2001 I've had a chance to teach a whole bunch of real-life law enforcement heroes, and I've even written another book for the law enforcement community. Here's the story:

Late in 2000, a high-ranking official from the FBI happened to hear me speak about the pursuit of spirituality. He was intrigued by my remarks, which, he told me later, were spiritual in nature without being too heavily religious. He explained that one unit within the FBI, which uses behavioral science to develop good police practices and techniques, was attempting to identify spiritual tools that could be used to combat severe stresses from which law enforcement officers suffer. They were looking for clergy who, without pushing a particular religious system, could help law enforcement officers connect spiritually.

He found my observations promising. But one talk by me wasn't much to go on. So he asked whether I had any experience or familiarity with law enforcement. I told him I'd been a prison chaplain for several years. Did I have any other materials that would let them know more about me, my interests, and my ability to contribute to this research of "identifying best practices of spirituality"? Was I sensitized to the unique realities and pressures that confront law enforcement officers?

I sent him a copy of my "Batman book" manuscript. He looked it over. Apparently it was authentically spiritual without being heavy-handedly religious, and it identified many of the themes that confront law enforcement officers. So he contacted me and invited me down to the FBI Academy in Quantico, Virginia.

I was invited on one condition: That I never mention Batman or any other "juvenile" ideas while I was there. Law enforcement officers aren't joking around, he explained, and they would, understandably, resent being told anything by a comic book-reading civilian! Someone else hinted to me gently that it wouldn't be a bad idea if I got a haircut before I came and wore a suit while at the Academy.

Thus began a five-year association with the FBI, during which time I have spoken and lectured and written at the FBI Academy. I have worked for a section of the FBI that conducts behavioral science research and provides cutting-edge resources for the larger law enforcement community. During these five years I have met, observed, listened to, and interviewed countless real-life heroic law enforcement officers.

I didn't rest on my Batman knowledge alone, of course. In preparation for my involvement with this project, I read thousands of pages on the topic of police stress. I familiarized myself with religious sources and what they might say to someone suffering such a stressful situation. The more I've read and the more I've listened and the more I've learned, the more I see that the insights I've developed flow from and rest solidly on the foundation that the Batman comics gave me.

I've attended and spoken at conferences held in Quantico on the topic of providing meaningful spiritual resources for law enforcement officers, not just FBI agents. As a result of my work and experiences with the FBI, I produced a book for law enforcement officers entitled *Spiritual Survival for Law Enforcement.*

I've learned a lot, too. Perhaps most of all, I have a newfound appreciation for and love of this simple book I offer you, *Wisdom from the Batcave.* At the end of the day, it still contains most of what I really want to share with the world, and which forms the bedrock of my approach to life. With all my admiration for the Batman, even I never really fully realized the power and universality of his message and what he stands for. This book is about recognizing the larger truths in a character of fiction.

When I first wrote it, I had hoped to teach "regular" people how to take these truths and apply them to their lives, how to be heroic in the course of "regular," everyday lives. I have had the supreme honor of discussing these truths with real-life heroic people who actually do all these things. Many of them do it on an intuitive level without even realizing what they do, and most of what I try to do is to make them aware of what they are and do. When I look at them carefully, I notice very few differences between them and the superheroes I have always loved to read about, even my beloved Batman.

I like to think of *Wisdom from the Batcave* as a civilian version of *Spiritual Survival for Law Enforcement*. I have tried to identify and present certain truths culled from both the Batman mythos and Jewish tradition that are relevant for you and me—everyday citizens who wield an enormous amount of power to change the world and make it a much better place.

Enjoy the book! Live its message!

PREFACE

As a child, my love of the Batman bordered on obsessive. My comic book collection, as well as my collection of Batman mugs, bowls, spoons, pens, lunch boxes, pajamas, slippers, watches, ties, key chains, wastebaskets, breakfast trays, sheets, alarm clocks, cookie jars, banks, posters, and, yes, Underoos™, was of astronomical proportion.

Far from attributing this fascination to childish whim, I have, in the wisdom of adulthood, come to understand it as related to something infinitely more profound. As an adult, I still enjoy the thrill of reading a Batman comic book for the first—or tenth—time. But now I have the additional thrill of being able to connect it to the most significant aspects of my life: my professional ambitions, my personal aspirations and my relationships with others.

If this seems like a tall order for even a superhero to fill, I suggest that you read on. You may find, as I did, that reading a comic book can be an enlightening experience, as well as one of the most enjoyable activities imaginable.

I am a rabbi and spend most of my time teaching classes on Torah ethics. My goal is to help people lead richer, more fulfilling lives. I've written several self-help books on practical Jewish ethics (using a computer with a Batman mouse pad and Batman screen saver, of course). In order to prepare for my job and to write those other books, I have spent innumerable years in college, graduate school, rabbinical school, and plain old everyday life studying ethics and morality, both in and out of a religious context.

Strangely enough, in the course of all this study, I have come to realize that a great deal of what I learned in these other settings, as well as what I teach in my various Torah classes, is information I first discovered on the pages of the Batman comic books. Coincidence? I believe not.

When I was a rabbi at Duke University a few years back, where most of this book was written, I would often find myself quoting a Batman comic book to clarify a point of Torah philosophy or ethics in a class or discussion. At first some students used to smirk or squirm in their chairs.

Before long they would expect me to look to the Batman to help illustrate ideas that we were discussing. Although they may have never read a Batman comic book or, more likely, wouldn't admit that they had, certain truths contained within the comic books resonated with them. Indeed, several of these students pressed me to commit these lessons to print.

Most of us are familiar with essays and books which analyze great, classic literary characters in order to determine what they represent and why they matter. Although my analysis is not always serious, I think the Batman has earned his place among these classic characters (many of whom he could easily best in a physical, even mental, contest). The ideals he represents, in addition to firing our imaginations, have the potential to inspire us to improve our lives and our relationships. And while it has always been a goal of my writing to help people learn how to live better, more moral lives, this book enables me to do so in the best possible way: through my great passion and deep reverence for the Batman.

What you hold in your hands, then, is the fruit of my childhood obsession. I hope you enjoy reading it as much as I have enjoyed writing it, and that it nourishes you as it has me. Don't forget to look at the pictures. And, by the way, I don't wear Underoos™ anymore. Haven't in about four years.

INTRODUCTION

Why Reading a Comic Book
is a Profound Experience

Every human being is endowed with a spiritual dimension—a soul—which contains an intuitive understanding of right and wrong, of good and evil. As we go through our lives, confronting people, situations and events, our souls have an innate ability to distinguish between the good guys and the bad guys. When we encounter moral truth, we recognize it as something we have seen before; it resonates within us. The point of education (whether book learning or just the school of hard knocks) is to bring this intuitive understanding to our consciousness and to teach us how to act upon it.

Since moral knowledge is already present in the human soul, moral education should be a fairly straightforward process. After all, it's teaching people something they already know, right? Wrong! In reality, teaching ethics and morality is usually difficult and frustrating. If this knowledge is already implanted in a young person, why should there be so much resistance to moral instruction?

Quite simply, people don't like being told what to do. No one appreciates a lecture. People respond defensively to preaching. This is particularly true of kids who know more than their parents do anyway. They want to live by values they have personally chosen and not ones which have been forced upon them by adults and other aliens.

Therein lies the great power of a story. Effective teachers use good stories to communicate complex ideas in ways that are not threatening or preachy. Before students even realize they are being lectured, before their defenses can go up, they get the message.

Comic book stories can play an important role in the process of moral education. They naturally address conflict between good and evil, right and wrong. In a light manner, comic book stories teach complex moral values. In addition, kids start reading comic books at a young age, which is the best time to start learning about morality and values. Lessons learned from reading comic books early on in life prepare a person for more formal teachings later on.

Comic book stories dramatize ideas and truths that we all intuitively recognize. Although these stories are not exactly "true," they nonetheless offer a kind of Truth that is more compelling than hard facts. And few comic book stories are more effective at laying the groundwork than the Batman.

In my own case, I learned many of the ideas in the pages that follow from the Bible and other primary religious texts while in yeshiva and rabbinical school. But to be honest I first encountered them in the Batman. When I was later presented with these same concepts in more formal settings, they seemed kind of familiar to me, as if I'd encountered them somewhere before. Years of Batman reading had prepared me to grasp complex philosophical concepts. Batman comics naturally affirm those things which we all most want to believe: that Good can ultimately triumph, albeit in dark and often mysterious ways.

When you read Batman comic books, along the way you may, as I did, learn some interesting facts, such as that the Battle of Hastings happened in 1066, belt-tongues of right-handed people point to the left, and that thallium is used in manufacturing glass.

More importantly, something deeper and much more profound emerges from these comic book stories: transcendent, universal lessons in how to deal with people, battle adversity, and become the heroes of our own—and even other people's—lives.

Who Is the Batman, Anyway?

I apologize for the absurd implication that there are people who do not know the particulars of the Batman's career and life. In the event of such an outrageous circumstance, here is a brief biography of the Batman.

Born to a life of wealth and leisure, eight-year-old Bruce Wayne was walking home from an evening at the movies with his parents, Dr. Thomas and Martha Wayne. The three were confronted by a gun-wielding hoodlum who stepped out of the shadows and demanded Martha's jewelry. A brief struggle ensued, after which the criminal shot and killed both Thomas and Martha Wayne right before young Bruce's eyes.

Leslie Thompkins was an elegant young woman at the time. She was in the fashionable Park Row neighborhood at the time of the murders, and was the first bystander to notice poor little Bruce Wayne. She held and comforted Bruce immediately after his parents' murder. Bruce went to live for some years with a great-uncle, Philip Wayne, who raised the boy to adulthood with the help of his servant, Alfred.

The shootings signaled the beginning of the end of Gotham City's Park Row neighborhood. Once-fashionable Park Row quickly declined into what would become grim, dangerous Crime Alley. And, of course, all the elegant, fashionable, high society types moved away—except Leslie Thompkins.

In another reality, Bruce might have grown up to sponsor gun-control legislation (the Wayne Bill) or created a support group for childhood victims of violent crimes. Bruce did neither. He responded in quite a different way. Traumatized by his parents' deaths, Bruce swore at their graveside to avenge their murders by dedicating the rest of his life to fighting crime.

> Batman comics naturally affirm those things which we all most want to believe: that Good can ultimately triumph, albeit in dark and often mysterious ways.

It was this very oath that propelled Bruce to devote every waking moment of his formative years to developing his mind and body to unparalleled perfection. Bruce traveled the world, during which he studied a wide variety of skills and disciplines that would later assist him in his chosen career.

After coming into his family inheritance, Bruce moved back into his family home, Wayne Manor, and pondered how best to fulfill his graveside vow. One night several weeks later, while sitting in the den of Wayne

Leslie Tompkins comforting young Bruce Wayne. (Detective Comics #457) © DC Comics

Manor, a large black bat suddenly flew in through an open window and startled Bruce.

This was the omen Bruce had been waiting for. Reasoning that criminals are a superstitious, cowardly lot, Bruce took his inspiration from the bat to design a costume that would strike fear into the hearts of evildoers everywhere. Thus was born a weird figure of the shadows...a dark avenger of evil...The Batman!

By day, Bruce maintains an image of a bored, idle playboy whose passion, if not talent, is golf. But the "playboy Bruce Wayne" persona is little more than a mask for Bruce's real identity as the Batman.

Why didn't Bruce just join the police department? One origin story explains that Bruce's one-time fiancée, Julie Madison, concerned for his safety, begged him not to endanger himself by becoming a police officer. Not content to take a desk job, Bruce invented this secret identity to save Julie from worry. The engagement was broken, but the secret identity and career remained.

Another theory is that something happened to convince Bruce that regular law enforcement officers are too constrained by the very laws that they seek to uphold and protect. This convinced him that a career as a policeman was not for him, and that he'd have to find some other way to fight for justice. That "other way" was to become the Batman.

Many decades ago, when this explanation was first proposed, one Batman origin story portrayed an exasperated Bruce Wayne bemoaning a legal system that makes it difficult for police officers to catch, and courts to prosecute, criminals. The Miranda ruling and other procedures governing proper search and seizure seemed to be endless obstacles to Bruce. The law appeared to be too soft to serve the interest of justice. That's where the Batman comes in. "I'm not interested in the law—I'm interested in justice," the Batman growls as he dangles a crook from the roof of a twenty-story building to convince him to reveal where his cohorts are. His civil rights violated, the crook nevertheless, talks— Bruce could never have done *that* as a policeman!

But times and society change, and everyone, even the Batman it seems, becomes more progressive. In a 1982 retelling of the story, Bruce decides not to become a policeman after a discussion in a law course in college. Supreme Court Justice Oliver Wendell Holmes, Jr. once reminded an attorney that "This is a court of law, young man, not a court of justice." Professor Rexford teaches Bruce that very same lesson in the following exchange between Professor Rexford and Bruce:

Professor Rexford: Two nineteen-year-old boys steal a car for a joy-ride! Along the way, one of them changes his mind, and asks to be let out of the car! Before his friend, who is driving, can comply, the car accidentally strikes an old woman crossing the street—and kills her! Should the boy who changed his mind still be charged with felony manslaughter, Mr. ... Wayne?

Bruce: Granted, the second boy stole the car, Professor—but he had no part in the accidental death! I would find him guilty of car theft—but not manslaughter!

Professor Rexford: And you would be wrong! Under the law, the second boy was just as guilty of complicity as if he had been behind the wheel!

Bruce: But is that justice, Professor Rexford?

The exchange concludes in the illustration below.

Bruce realized that the law can be too harsh, and does not serve the interest of justice. That's where the Batman—soft, compassionate, liberal Batman!—comes in. It's a little bit of a (politically correct) stretch.

During the Batman's 60 years of existence, each team of writers and artists has focused on particular aspects of the character. Each creative team's vision has differed, and each decade has had its own Batman.

Professor Rexford's class motivates Bruce to pursue justice in unconventional ways.
(Untold Legend of the Batman) © DC Comics

The ideas that follow are not derived from any one comic book story-line or any particular era or any particular writer/artist team. These are, instead, the *fundamental ideas* or, rather, the *universal Truths* that define the heart-and-soul of the Batman character. These ideas define the essential character of the Batman, and go to the heart of why he is one of popular literature's most enduring, captivating and, ultimately, inspirational figures.

These ideas raise the Batman from a mere two-dimensional comic-book character to become a larger-than-life hero, symbol and inspiration.

Here then, in the pages that follow, are some of the great lessons I learned from reading Batman.

CHAPTER 1

The Blessing of Family

His parents' murder is the central defining event of Bruce Wayne's life—everything flows from it. Whatever Bruce Wayne does is driven by that void in his life, by that sense of loss and rage at having been denied his parents, from having grown up without their love and guidance.

The loss of his parents is so powerful that it provides a lifetime of inspiration for Bruce's difficult, grueling work. It haunts him every moment of every day of his life, and drives him to train tirelessly and fight relentlessly to ensure that no one else will ever suffer in the same way.

Dick Grayson (the first and greatest Robin) was also orphaned as a young boy after criminals killed his parents. In Robin Annual #4, he speaks for Bruce, as well, when he describes a childhood characterized by little other than "the pain, the loss, the loneliness."

Did you ever notice that people rarely appreciate what they have until they don't have it anymore? Loss is often the first step in appreciating the great gifts in our lives.

It is a sad reality that few of us appreciate our blessings until they disappear.

Imagine what Bruce would give to have had his parents present to nurture him while he was growing up. He would have gladly foregone all that he has achieved and accomplished, all the good he has done, to have had the love and warmth of his parents, Thomas and Martha. A recurring theme in the Batman stories is the importance of family, the blessing of parents and children nurturing and loving one another.

Many of us fantasize about wealth, power and fame. If we could only…win the lottery, play for the NBA, sit in the White House, be a superhero…

What does Bruce Wayne fantasize about?

In "Perchance to Dream," an episode of *Batman: The Animated Series* (Fox Kids Network, Airdate: 10/19/92), the Mad Hatter captures the Batman and places him in an ideal imaginary dreamworld that he could never want to leave. What does the Batman dream about? What seductive vision does he conjure up? A very mundane existence, with his parents alive and well. He fantasizes about nothing more grandiose or elaborate than to have his family. What Bruce dreams about is, actually, commonplace and mundane for most of us.

The lesson is clear. We may not have Bruce's financial success or his incomparable talents, but we are blessed with loving relationships. Even though our parents, siblings, children, spouses and in-laws are imperfect, they are still forces of love and support in a lonely world. They care about us, worry about our safety and health. Bruce would trade all of his fame and fortune for a chance to have such relationships.

Think what a happy place the world would be if we recognized that *we already have* what we really want and need in life. What if the things we dreamed about were the ones that could really bring us lasting peace?

> Blessings that go unrecognized go unappreciated.

What if, instead of fantasizing about money, glory and our adoring public, we dreamed of growing old with our spouses, watching our grandchildren grow and develop? Those are wishes that are within our grasp. But more importantly, they are wishes that bring lasting contentment, and not mere fleeting pleasures.

A great advantage of comic book fiction—indeed, any fiction—is that you can imagine and test out possibilities that are unlikely or impossible in the everyday universe as we experience it.

Back in 1994, the entire DC Comics universe experienced the "zero-hour" phenomenon, which caused a series of time anomalies; and, for a brief period, Thomas and Martha Wayne were alive again. Let's look at Bruce's reaction to the news that his parents were alive, if only briefly.

Our sequence begins with Bruce's realization that his parents are alive at Wayne Manor. He, of course, rushes back to see them, and, after his car is wrecked, resorts to running the last mile to return home to them.

Is that *really* his "every dream answered" described in Figure 1-1 — "To hear my father's voice, to feel my mother's embrace"?

It sure is. From very simple experiences come profound pleasures.

As parents, we must be constantly aware of the gift and the responsibility of nurturing our children. Bruce's loss of parental love caused him lifelong pain and yearning. Our ability to be present in our children's lives, to express our love for them, and to help guide them into adulthood is a gift never to be taken for granted. It is our voices, our embraces that mean so much to our children.

Figure 1-1: Bruce's excitement at the thought of seeing his parents once again. (Detective Comics #678) © DC Comics

Figure 1-2: Nightwing teaching Robin not to take a gift for granted. (Robin #8) © DC Comics

That's what Nightwing tries to teach Robin in the exchange in Figure 1-2. Tim Drake (the third and present Robin) is complaining to a grown Dick Grayson (the original Robin, now the hero Nightwing) about his need to come up with excuses to explain his crime-fighting-related absences to his father.

Tim's complaint sounds familiar to us. How often do we complain about overbearing, nagging parents? How many jokes do we make about the guilt our parents inspire in us?

Dick's response is bracing: What he wouldn't give to "have someone to lie to" — *i.e.,* parents who care for and worry about him!

Growing up with parents and siblings, even imperfect ones, is a blessing. If we complain about them at times, we also know how empty life would be without them. So instead of waiting until those blessings are no longer in our lives, why not pick up the phone today, and rediscover how great it is to have "someone to lie to."

Sometimes in life our natural family does not provide us with the nurturing we need. Divorce, illness and death all conspire to rob us of those precious relationships we need so desperately. In his own way, Bruce created a surrogate family to recreate some of what was lost. For a loner, the Batman has done an amazing job filling up the Batcave! His family consists of Alfred Pennyworth, Dick Grayson, Commissioner Gordon, Leslie Thompkins, Tim Drake, Barbara Gordon, and many others.

The Batman teaches us that when circumstances require it, we can create a family to replace the one that should be there to provide us with the emotional warmth and nourishment we need. In characteristic fashion, the Batman identifies a need—emotional support—and rather than crying about what's missing he constructs a reality for himself to meet that need.

CHAPTER 2

How to Triumph over Adversity

A s a young boy, Bruce Wayne was dealt the cruelest blow imaginable. He watched as his parents were murdered before his eyes!
What greater horror can a child endure?

My mother and most of her friends are survivors of the Holocaust.
They witnessed unspeakable atrocities directed both at themselves and at
the people closest to them. As a child, I would listen to their stories. What
always amazed me was the way they responded to their tragedies. My
Mom and her friends came to this country with absolutely nothing. By
the time I arrived on the scene, they had married, raised families, built
businesses and sent their kids to college.

People respond differently to tragedies. Some people succumb to despair
and self-pity. A typical response is "Why me? I just can't go on." Others dig
deep and find a reservoir of inner strength they never knew they had.

After his parents' cold-blooded murder, Bruce could easily have allowed
himself to hide behind a thick curtain of denial for the rest of his life. His
inherited wealth would have allowed him to drown himself in materialis-
tic, mind-numbing pleasure. He could have become the
lazy, selfish, mindless playboy he only pretends to be.
Who would have blamed him?

Instead, Bruce Wayne chose a very different path. He
refused—and refuses—to succumb to despair or to
embrace a philosophy of hopelessness. Every day—
indeed, every moment—of his life, he faces squarely
the adversity that life has dealt him, and he triumphs
over it spectacularly.

> Every day—indeed,
> every moment—of his
> life, he faces squarely
> the adversity that life
> has dealt him, and he
> triumphs over it spec-
> tacularly.

Obviously, he can't bring his parents back to life. So
what does it mean to win? He takes the miserable situation life handed him and, unbroken and defiant, con-
verts it into magnificent victory by working, constantly
and tirelessly, to ensure that no one else suffers such senseless loss.

Spiraling into despair was not an option for Bruce. Figure 2-1 describes
what Bruce Wayne chose to do as a result of his own experience with
tragedy.

Many of us suffer misfortunes in our lives. We, too, can choose how to
respond.

It's so easy and seductive to succumb to depression and wallow in self-
pity, to talk forevermore about what might have been "if only." The true test
of heroism is to refuse to surrender to despair, to face squarely the difficulties that confront us and to try to impose a little order on our messy lives.

Figure 2-1: Batman using his own experience with tragedy to spare others a similar fate. (Detective Comics #0) © DC Comics

Self-pity is the easy way out. The more difficult choice is the road that the Batman chooses. His loss is ever before his eyes, the wound reopened daily. It would be much easier to bury his pain in some self-indulgent, self-defeating behavior.

Jewish tradition teaches that This World is a preparation for the Next World, a world of the spirit. Our job in This World, then, is to prepare for the Next World by developing and refining our character. While this can be a painful process, our goal is to challenge ourselves to rise above adversity and become the best, most noble version of ourselves.

Misfortune creates opportunities for personal growth, development and refinement of character.

Would Mahatma Gandhi, Michael Collins, Menachem Begin or Martin Luther King, Jr. have found the strength within themselves to change the world if not for the adversity they confronted? Would Helen

Generating some light, even if it's only a little bit, begins to dispel the darkness that surrounds us. Sometimes the biggest challenge we face is to overcome our own internal demons. Heroism means taking control of negative circumstances and converting them into positive ones.

Keller have attained the same greatness of character if not for her physical disabilities and her determination to triumph over them?

When life is easy, and everything is comfortable, there may be no particular need to tap into the depths of our potential. Why should we? It doesn't require a lot of bravery or patience to endure an ice cream sandwich of happiness and comfort.

Smooth seas do not make skillful sailors.
– African proverb

On the other hand, when adversity strikes, we often begin to contemplate the preciousness of health and life and what we could be accomplishing. If Thomas and Martha had not been murdered, Bruce may have become the indolent, shallow, spoiled playboy he only now pretends to be. What motivation would he have had to tap into those limitless capabilities and push himself tirelessly to help people and battle evil? Why would he bother?

🦇 🦇 🦇

In the classic Detective Comics #500, a shadowy, supernatural hero, the Phantom Stranger, offers the Batman a chance to travel to another, alternate reality to prevent the murder and save the lives of Thomas and Martha Wayne. Robin [Dick Grayson] accompanies the Batman on this

Rachel is a woman who volunteers at the Duke University Medical Center, counseling families of brain cancer patients. She is sensitive, genuinely concerned, and understanding. It is breathtaking to watch her in action.

Once, after watching her in a particularly difficult interaction with a family, I complimented her on her work. "How do you do it?" I asked. "How did you get such sensitivity, such insight?"

"My daughter died of brain cancer when she was in her twenties," she explained, "and I've been exactly where these families are now. I know exactly what these families are going through. Who better than I to comfort them and give them strength?" This woman is a hero the Batman would admire. Like Bruce Wayne, she turned what was surely the saddest event of her life into an opportunity to nurture and comfort others who are experiencing similar pain.

journey into that other dimension which lags behind ours by about twenty years, at the point when the Waynes are approaching their encounter with the gunman.

The Batman and Robin observe the Waynes of this other dimension in their home. The Batman, of course, is overwhelmed to see his "parents," and his reaction is obvious: "I swear by all that's dear to me... I won't let you die again!" What's not obvious is Robin's reaction. He is circumspect because the young Bruce Wayne of this dimension is a "spoiled little brat!" Consider Robin's analysis in Figure 2-2.

Bruce Wayne used his own experience with personal tragedy to ensure that other people would live happier lives.

A crushing tragedy isn't the only way to inspire growth and accomplishment. Before we consider other lessons to be learned from the Batman, let's return for a moment to the happy conclusion of Detective Comics #500:

The Batman and Robin successfully prevent the murder of that realm's Thomas and Martha Wayne. But what becomes of little "spoiled brat" Bruce? Apparently, we learn from the story's postscript in Figure 2-3, adversity doesn't have to be final or fatal to knock us out of our complacency.

Robin ponders what might have been if Bruce's parents had lived.
(Detective Comics #500)
© DC Comics

Let's use the small reminders and opportunities for growth, and maybe we won't ever have to receive those bigger, more permanent, less pleasant ones.

Figure 2-3: The Bruce of another dimension uses his brush with tragedy to become a hero. (Detective Comics #500) © DC Comics

Tragedy, catastrophic events, and wicked people serve an important function: They provide resistance against which we struggle and strive in order to refine and elevate ourselves. The battle against evil is a motivation that ennobles us by demanding that we reach inward and find a will and the resolve to struggle against evil and injustice. If there were no such challenges, we might never turn inward and find that resolve, strength of will and character needed to fight evil—and we would never become spiritually great in the process.

It is, perhaps, a troubling truth that we do not turn inward and find the greatness within ourselves until we must confront catastrophic events and the basest wickedness of other people. Faced with no challenge, we can become lazy and complacent. When danger—and the greatest danger is the myriad expressions of human evil and wickedness—threatens, we turn inward and tap into unbelievable reservoirs of strength, resolve, conviction and decency. If life provides opportunities to sink to the depths of depravity that we can sink to when we exercise free will to choose evil, it also provides opportunities to attain the heights of nobility to which people can rise when we exercise our free will to choose good.

CHAPTER 3

Recognizing the Extent of Human Potential

O ne of the most pervasive themes of Jewish religious tradition is the endless capacity for human greatness. Not surprisingly, this is a constant message of Batman comic books: *How far does human potential extend?* The Batman stories are unequivocally clear: to infinity. There is no limit.

This lesson about the endless capability of every human being is the single most important theme of Batman. It is this greatest of all truths that defines the essence of the Batman and accounts for his enduring appeal. The Batman, more than any other literary character, reminds us that every person has an infinite capacity for achievement.

**If we do not realize that potential, it is only because
we do not believe we have it. But it's there, all the same.**

A Hasidic story is told of the famous Rabbi Zusia, who spent his life focused on improving his personal character traits. Once, when Rabbi Zusia and his brother had been traveling for many days without food or shelter and they were exhausted and famished, they lay down by the side of the road to rest for a short while, and Rabbi Zusia's brother promptly fell asleep.

Rabbi Zusia noticed a wagon coming toward them. The wagon was filled with bales of hay. Every time the wagon reached a bump in the road, one of the bales would fall to the ground. The driver would stop his wagon, climb down, lift the heavy bale of hay, throw it back on top, and climb back onto the wagon.

As luck would have it, a bale of hay fell to the ground just when the wagon passed Rabbi Zusia. The wagon driver yelled, "Hey, you! Pick up the hay and throw it back on." Rabbi Zusia, relating the incident some time later, said that at that moment he could barely imagine lifting himself up, let alone picking up the bale of hay. He called back, "I can't. I'm too weak." With that the wagon driver angrily retorted, *"You can. You just don't want to."*

Rabbi Zusia said that of all the ethical literature he had studied, this was the most profound ethical statement he had ever heard. For the rest of his life, whenever he imagined that something was too hard for him to accomplish, he remembered the words of the wagon driver: *"You can. You just don't want to."*

If we don't do the things that Batman does, nevertheless, something inside us resonates to the stories and whispers that we *could*—if we only majored in chemistry, worked out hard enough, learned kung fu, studied acrobatics, practiced rappelling, apprenticed to racecar drivers, demolition experts, crossbow experts, contortionists and master detectives. Mastery of each skill is within the realm of possibility; human beings have certainly excelled and mastered these disciplines, and many more besides.

But we are used to seeing a person excel in only one area, if at all. How can we master two difficult disciplines, let alone twenty or thirty? The lesson of the Batman is that human potential is enormous. Anything is possible if we utilize all—or, at least, more—of our capabilities. We get a glimpse of this every once in a while when we hear of an adrenaline-fueled mother who single-handedly picked up the front of a car so her child, pinned beneath, could crawl out.

> *Do not pray for tasks equal to your powers; pray for powers equal to your tasks.*
> – Bishop Phillips Brooks

We can. We just have to want to.

Modern research and timeless religion teach us that we don't even begin to tap into the potential we possess in our souls, minds and bodies. A great sage once commented, *"The greatest danger for most of us is not that we set our goals too high and fail to reach them; the problem is that we set our goals too low and we reach them."*

This is certainly the lesson of the Batman. His goals seem lofty to us—yet without such grand goals, he would never have accomplished even a quarter of the greatness of which he is capable.

Figure 3-1: Bruce pursuing mental and physical perfection. (Batman #47) © DC Comics

Germany's Kaiser Wilhelm was on board a ship when one of his sailors fell overboard. The sailor panicked and flailed around in the water, screaming for help. "Help me!" the sailor shouted, "I don't know how to swim!" Shipmates tried to throw him a rope, but in his panic he had started drifting farther and farther away.

The kaiser came upon the scene, drew his pistol and took aim at the panic-stricken young man. "You swim back to this boat or I'll blow your brains out," he roared.

Flailing and thrashing ungracefully, the sailor nevertheless managed to make it back to the ship. A soft-spoken, thoughtful man, the kaiser helped the sailor aboard.

Don't be afraid to make demands on yourself and push yourself beyond the comfortable limits of what you think you can accomplish; you'll never exhaust your reservoir of potential for accomplishment and achievement. The only limits we possess are the ones we impose upon ourselves.

A great rabbi used to say, *"I never asked myself if I could do it. I only asked myself if it needed to be done."* In his relentless struggle against evil, the Batman never asks himself if he can do it; he asks only if it needs to be done.

In our lives there are superhuman feats that need to be accomplished. Whether it's loving an unlovable grouch, imparting values to a malevolent teenager, caring for a burdensome parent, let's not ask ourselves if we can do it; let's just find out if it needs to be done.

CHAPTER 4

The Value of Willpower

Each of us possesses an endless—indeed, infinite—potential for greatness. But possessing potential and realizing it are two completely different stories. There is a lot of work in between. There are many cold, rainy mornings at 5 A.M. when you just don't feel like getting out of a comfortable bed and running for an hour, and it's hard to remember, when you're at 499, why pushup number 500 is so important. Believing, or even knowing, that you can do it is one thing. Exercising the willpower to get it done is quite another.

Willpower means sacrificing some ease and comfort right now for a greater goal sometime later. Willpower is stubbornness: It is refusing to give up when you encounter difficulty.

You can't get through life in any meaningful way without it. Asked to define a "strong man," a Talmudic sage explained that the only person who can be described as strong is one who is in control of himself. There is no strength that is not inner strength, no power that is not inner power. All outer strength is false and illusory. Real strength flows from inside outward. All the outer trappings of power are nothing if the person who possesses them is weak inside.

Figure 4-1: Robin (Tim Drake) explains the secret of the Batman's success. (Gotham Adventures #25)
© *DC Comics*

Willpower is indispensable to the success of any endeavor. You'll never realize your goal, other than the most trivial, without it. Without willpower, we easily get distracted and discouraged. The slightest bump in the road is enough to derail our plans and upset our focus. Some people do set worthwhile, challenging goals for themselves, but run out of steam before reaching them. That's where most of us end up: just shy of the finish line.

Certainly it is Bruce Wayne's willpower that has made him what he is. His will is indomitable; he never wavers for a moment.

> There is no strength that is not inner strength, no power that is not inner power.

How did Bruce Wayne keep plugging away at it, for so long? Where does that strength of will come from?

Some people naturally possess great willpower; nothing gets in the way of their goals. But you *can* develop it. You develop willpower in the same way you build a strong muscle – by exercising it often. How many of us ever say "no" to ourselves?

Here's a simple exercise to get you started: Eat one potato chip, then close the bag. You're on your way!

If you have a worthy goal, stay with it, tenaciously, until you succeed. Don't allow yourself to be distracted by every little (or big) diversion that comes your way. Commit yourself to do anything legally and morally correct to succeed. And ask God for help.

Bruce's willpower is fueled by rage over his parents' deaths. But it is also propelled by something else. Look closely at the oath he took so long ago, reproduced in Figure 4-2 below.

I prefer this particular presentation of the oath Bruce took because it introduces an element absent in other retellings of his origin: the term

Figure 4-2: A mixture of rage and faith provides Bruce with unending willpower. (Secret Origins #6) © DC Comics

Make and Take Your Oath

Oaths can be very effective at keeping us focused on a goal and prevent us from becoming discouraged in its pursuit. Oaths possess a spiritual, transcendent quality that directs our thoughts away from the world of the concrete and material and toward the world of the spirit, toward the world of ideas.

I get a thrill every time the Batman's Justice League teammate Hal Jordan recharges his power ring to become the Green Lantern: "In brightest day, in blackest night, no evil shall escape my sight. Let those who worship evil's might beware my power: Green Lantern's light!"

Consider the fateful scene in which the Batman administered the oath to Dick Grayson before he could become Robin. Dick Grayson's hand was on the Bible, and the Batman instructed him: "Swear by all that is holy that you will never deviate from the path of justice."

Construct your own oath. Say it daily.

Unromantic types call such an oath a "mission statement." They talk about "core values." What are your core values? Write a mission statement for your life. You don't have one, you say? You just go with the flow, wherever it carries you, with no clearly stated defined goals? You're in serious danger.

Write your mission statement. Laminate it. Read it every morning.

"dear God." I'd like to think that has something to do with his success. Maybe he's been able to maintain his resolve because he considers his cause a religious duty, his personal means of serving God.

Willpower is essential, but it only goes so far. It is the human ingredient in success. We each have to do our part. But ultimate success comes with God's blessings. Bruce Wayne coupled his indomitable will with simple, basic prayer. No matter how strong our willpower, success comes only from Him. But we have to make our best attempt before we can look to Him to make it happen.

Steve Englehart: Batman's the greatest of the heroes because he's the purest — it's just a guy and his desire. No super-powers, just a refusal to lose. He's what any one of us could be if we dedicated ourselves the way he did. It's that dedication that keeps him from being crazy, which is an argument I've had to deal with from the start. He knows if he slipped over the edge he'd become less effective, and he's all about being effective. (Quoted in *Sequential Tart*)

CHAPTER 5

The Value of Hard Work

I f Bruce Wayne is the Batman, it is due to a lifetime of hard, grueling, backbreaking work, both physical and mental. That's the only way to succeed. You have to pay your dues – in the gym, and in the library.

Most of us, raised on a steady diet of instant gratification, are frightened when we consider pursuing a goal that will take us years of effort to complete.

Many of us are dissuaded from beginning, from taking that first step, because it will take twenty years to reach the goal. But someday we'll be twenty years older anyway, God willing! Wouldn't it be nice to be twenty years older and have accomplished the goal?

Most of us want to sweep in at the spectacular finish, where all the glory seems to be, but those finishes must be earned. There are no short-

Figure 4-2: Batman demonstrates the result of hard work and preparation. (Detective Comics #704) © DC Comics

When I was a teenager, I considered studying a particular form of martial arts, but was told that it would take seven years of intense training to complete the beginner's course. I decided seven years was too long to wait to get what I wanted, so I never started. That was over twenty years ago! (I actually started the course about three years ago, right after I finished this manuscript. I was inspired by this lesson!)

cuts—no yellow sun or earth's lesser gravity, no radioactive spider, and no gamma radiation. Bruce wasn't born physically or mentally perfect. He fought for each additional skill and discovery. And his work never ends. His skills require constant maintenance and improvement. Each case demands hours of research, cross-checking, and just plain waiting. None of that stuff is very glamorous, but that's the only way to succeed.

One of the main differences between the Batman and other super-heroes is his recognition that, in life, greatness must be earned. It is not magically bestowed.

Worthy goals require hard work. Hard work builds character, even as it builds other skills or muscles. Be suspicious of goals that don't make demands of you. They probably aren't worthy of you, and they probably aren't worth attaining

Don't be fooled by how easy the Batman makes it all look, when he sweeps in to save the day. A lot of hard work went into that "effortless" victory! In fact, the more preparation, the more effortless the final victory seems.

What you are is God's gift to you; what you make of it is your gift to God."
—Rev. Anthony Dalla Villa

CHAPTER 6

A Better Definition
of Victory

Sometimes it seems that the only victories that really matter are the ones that take place on a grand scale: winning an Olympic gold medal, a Grammy, Emmy or Oscar. That's not true. What we accomplish locally, on the small scale, matters, too. The Talmud teaches, "He who saves a single life, it is as though he has saved an entire world." What this means is that the single person whose life is saved represents an entire world to the people who are close to her and the generations of descendants that might exist in the future because her life was saved. The Batman's massive accomplishments are exciting, but for each individual person or family whose life has been affected by the Batman, the only episode that matters is the one they're in.

Although the Batman knows that he is not going to rid the world, much less Gotham City, of evil, he understands the value in each individual act of heroism he performs. When he saves a man's life—a man who is a husband, father, or son—does the fact that evil is being done (or will be done) somewhere else minimize the happiness of his wife, child or parent who has been spared so much sorrow, whose life would otherwise have been irrevocably, tragically altered?

In Detective Comics #568, Robin (Jason Todd) questions the Batman's judgment in leaving him to tend to a wounded person.

Identify Your "Starfish"

A story is told about a little boy walking by the shore. He makes his way gingerly along the beach, being careful to avoid the thousands of starfish that have been washed up onto the shore. He notices a man in the distance who is busily throwing starfish back into the water.

The boy approaches the man. "What are you doing?" he asks.

Without stopping his work, the man replies, "Just what it looks like—I'm throwing the starfish back into the water before they die."

"But don't you realize that you'll never be able to throw them all back in?" the boy asks incredulously. "There are thousands of them!?"

"Does it matter that I can't save them all? I saved this one, and this one, and this one, and this one..."

Robin asks, "But the police can take care of that! Why do you always leave me behind for all the unimportant stuff?"

Figure 6-1 depicts the Batman's response.

Victory does not have to be defined in grand, absolute terms.
We cannot feed the world; but we can feed one hungry person who
lives in our community. And that is a victory of cosmic proportions.

Goals need not be gigantic or absolute to be worthwhile. Some goals are so high as to be unreachable. Instead, let's see victory in one act of kindness, one act of heroism or selflessness. Helping one human being, even if it's your own spouse or parent, can be as heroic as stopping a runaway train.

Figure 6-1: Batman providing a more mature definition
of victory. (Detective Comics #568) © DC Comics

Keep a diary, a daily account of your benevolent acts and the people you have helped. Total up your account on a monthly and yearly basis to keep track of how you're really doing.

It's not necessary to set a hard-and-fast quota. Rather, the idea is to recognize, and enjoy, each individual act for what it is: a stunning victory. Every day has at least one victory, and probably many. True, there are still lots of starfish out there waiting to be touched by you. You'll get to them. For the moment, though, think about the ones you helped today. There will be plenty of time to think about those other ones later. Right now, find your starfish for today.

CHAPTER 7

The Value of
Inspiring Others

A person is capable of accomplishing amazing things. There is practically no limit to what any one of us is capable of accomplishing. While each individual act is enormous, the cumulative effect of many years of effort is earth-shattering.

But it doesn't end there. Our lives have astounding value far beyond what we personally accomplish.

What was Bruce Wayne thinking during all those years of lonely, tireless training? What ambitions did he have? Did he have aspirations of fighting all the villains in the world, of vanquishing all evil, for all time?

Probably not. He's not insane. What, then, drove him? Didn't he realize the futility of his work? What, after all, can one man or woman do?

Such individuals provide inspiration for countless others, in their generation and for all time. Obviously, the Batman knows that he will not—cannot—rid the world, or even Gotham City, of evil. But his behavior sets an example to others to work for justice, to end misery, to battle evil and not stand by idly.

There is value to what every person does beyond his or her obvious, direct accomplishments. Throughout history, in the darkest times, there have been individuals who served as symbols of what a human being can aspire to. During the Holocaust, Raoul Wallenberg, a Swedish diplomat who was not Jewish, supplied Swedish passports to as many as 20,000 Hungarian Jews and saved them from being deported to Nazi death camps. During his last rescue mission, he was taken into custody by Russian army officers, and no one is really sure what happened to him.

It's true that Raoul Wallenberg was directly responsible for saving thousands of lives. That alone is an act of astounding significance. But how many little boys like me grew up hearing about the heroic role that Raoul Wallenberg played? As a child of a Holocaust survivor, I knew about evil from an early age. Imagine what it meant to me and my little friends to know that the opposite of evil was Raoul Wallenberg? His effect went far beyond the 20,000 lives he saved.

Chaos, indifference, irresponsibility, selfishness, fear and evil all threaten our society; the Batman imposes order, demonstrates concern, assumes responsibility, practices selflessness and self-sacrifice, shows resolve and confidence to battle, and champions justice.

The Batman represents the best of human resolve, will, sacrifice, strength, justice and courage – all that is most nobly human, most genuinely spiritual. He inspires the citizenry of Gotham City (and we are all citizens of Gotham City). It is significant that the word "inspire" is derived from the word "spirit": the Batman infuses the community he serves with a measure of his own noble spirit, and the community partakes of his spiritual strength.

Where once the citizens of Gotham City might have been overwhelmed, paralyzed by fear, cowed by malevolence, and disillusioned, instead—*because of the Batman*—they are comforted, inspired and strengthened.

> *All that is necessary for the triumph of evil is for good men to do nothing.*
> —Attributed to Edmund Burke

> *Each time a man stands for an ideal, or acts to improve the lot of others, or strikes out against injustice, he sends forth a tiny ripple of hope.*
> —Robert F. Kennedy

Many times Bruce Wayne has remarked that he was inspired during his youth by the heroic deeds of other, earlier crusaders for justice, among them Zorro, the Shadow and the Gray Ghost. It's good to be inspired.

We can be inspired by other people, but we don't always have the opportunity to meet our heroes personally. The Batman is fortunate to have met several of his inspirations.

Batman #253 describes the Batman's first meeting with the Shadow. The Batman has been tracking some counterfeiters, and so, apparently, has the Shadow. The panels in Figure 7-1 describe the two heroes meeting after the case has been successfully solved, with the counterfeiting ring broken up and the criminals arrested. The Batman wonders why, after all these years, the Shadow has chosen to come out of retirement and resume his crime-fighting career. Figure 7-1 shows the exchange between these two titans.

My pulse quickens every time I read this simple yet elegant exchange.

In "Beware the Gray Ghost," an episode of *Batman: The Animated Series* (Fox Kids Network, Airdate: 11/4/92), the Batman teams up with Simon Trent, the actor who portrayed the Gray Ghost on TV many years

Figure 7-1: The Batman meets his childhood inspiration. (Batman #253) © DC Comics

earlier, when Bruce Wayne was a boy. Trent is an actor, and an aging one at that, who is somewhat resentful toward the Gray Ghost character. It seems he was typecast decades ago because of his portrayal of the TV superhero, and as a result could not get other acting jobs after the series ended. For all these reasons, he is reluctant to take part in a potentially dangerous criminal investigation of Gray Ghost-theme related robberies.

After a change of heart, Trent dons his old Gray Ghost costume and aids the Batman in his investigation, and even saves the Batman's life at one point, demonstrating that he really was worthy to portray that noble TV character. In gratitude, the Batman brings Trent to the Batcave—"almost an exact replica of the Gray Ghost's Lair," Trent notes—and the Batman shows Trent the shrine to the Gray Ghost he built in the Batcave. "As a boy, I used to watch you with my father. The Gray Ghost was my hero."

Forgotten are the years of unemployment, obscurity, and poverty. Simon Trent realizes that he accomplished something infinitely bigger and more important: He inspired a small boy to grow up to be a hero. "So it wasn't all for nothing," says Trent. What greater happiness, or success, could anyone ask for?

Note a significant difference between these two inspirations: For Bruce Wayne, the Shadow was a real-life crusader for justice while the Gray Ghost was a TV hero portrayed by an actor. Nevertheless, both inspired a little boy for a lifetime.

In Figure 7-2, Commissioner Gordon reflects on the Batman's influence on his own and his daughter's lives. (Commissioner Gordon's daughter Barbara became Batgirl!)

Sometimes we look at a task and the effort seems too great—greater than we can do ourselves. How do we approach such a situation? Despair is never an option. But what to do? The task looks enormous. The Talmud reminds us, "It's not up to you to finish the job, but you have to at least make a start."

There are many times in life when we become paralyzed as we think about how much work lies ahead. Responsibilities pile up and feel like a burden. The Talmud is teaching us, don't worry about the end. Make your start. The easiest, surest way for evil to win is for good, moral people to do nothing. Maybe you'll make a sizable dent in the work. And when you yourself can do no more, know that you can take great credit for, and satisfaction in, the fact that your personal example has inspired others to continue the work. That's what the Shadow and Simon Trent (the TV Gray Ghost) think whenever they hear about the Batman's exploits.

Figure 7-2: The Batman inspired so many others to do good. (Untold Legend of the Batman)
© DC Comics

> In the course of our lives, each of us encounters situations in which we can accomplish greatness. But what we do has so much more impact because we provide the inspiration for others to follow. If a person can inspire a thousand (or even only three) others to do something right, this is a great accomplishment: The deeds of one person are magnified manyfold.

Bruce Wayne was clearly aware of this capacity and of the necessity to inspire others, as his musings in Figure 7-3 indicate.

Each one of us can become that "rallying point" for others through the compelling example of our own work, dedication and selflessness. We might surprise even ourselves. Raoul Wallenberg had no idea what he set in motion when he issued that first passport to freedom. Even more importantly, somebody somewhere—a parent, a teacher, perhaps—inspired him to become the great person he was. That person's name may be forgotten from history, but her legacy lives on.

Recognize that you are a symbol.

You can be a symbol—of hope against the chaos that threatens civilization and would engulf it in a moment if you were not there. As you were inspired, so too you inspire others who will take up the mantle and practice decency and heroism in their private lives.

Figure 7-3: Bruce Wayne pondering the power of inspiring others. (Untold Legend of the Batman) © DC Comics

CHAPTER 8

The Value of Self-Esteem

How can we account for Bruce Wayne's ability to stand around at society parties and act like a total fool? Even more, how can he stand there while everyone is berating the Batman, decrying his vigilante tactics, impugning his motives and honesty? In fact, Bruce doesn't just stand there silently while this is happening—he joins them in condemning his alter ego! How can he do it? How could anyone summon up the self-control necessary to play this role?

In fact, it's not hard for Bruce to do it at all, and no real self-control is required. Why? Because Bruce Wayne couldn't care less about other people's opinions about him, in either of his identities.

If we heard ourselves spoken of in this way, most of us would not be able to endure it; we would have to defend ourselves and attack those whose righteous indignation comes at our expense. But not the Batman. He knows what he is and what he does. He doesn't need other people to know it, too. His assessment of what he does is not influenced by other people's opinions. What freedom!

In fact, if he were to pursue acknowledgment, recognition or glory, it would undermine and destroy his effectiveness in his mission. That's probably true for most of us, whether we realize it or not. When you are truly at peace with who and what you are, what other people say about you doesn't matter at all.

> Most of us spend our lives trying to convince the world of our worth, in the hope that we ourselves will finally believe it.

Most people become frustrated, resentful, incensed and outraged when the world around them refuses to acknowledge their importance and honor them in the way they imagine they deserve. They believe that if they were given acknowledgment and praise they would be at peace. It's not true. Like a drug, the need for affirmation from others is addictive: the more you get, the more you need.

Most of us spend our lives trying to convince the world of our worth, in the hope that we ourselves will finally believe it. That pursuit can only end in frustration and failure, because unless we truly value ourselves, we'll never really convince anyone else of our worth.

Even if by chance we succeed in convincing some people, we won't convince everyone, and the ones we don't will trouble us and deprive us of a sense of victory, because these holdouts tend to confirm our own hidden fears about our worthlessness and inadequacies. And, if, by some miracle, we manage to succeed in convincing the whole world, it still won't do one bit of good. The whole world shouting our praises won't be able to drown out that loudest voice of all: the one inside ourselves.

If, however, you develop a strong inner sense of self and recognize your own value, you won't need anybody's praise to make you feel good (and you'll still be able to enjoy it if it happens to come your way). A strong sense of self and self-worth should not be confused with vanity or arrogance, which are often simply masks to hide inner doubt. Rather, I am talking about a healthy self-knowledge and sense of pride in your own positive attributes and accomplishments.

The only person who has to be convinced of your worth as a human being is you. The world's opinion of you, for good or bad, is incidental. While it is nice for others to applaud your successes, in the long run these opinions are of small value. Efforts to garner public acceptance often come at the expense of those things that are really important to you.

How does a person acquire a sense of self worth? Living by the values described in this book is a good start. In short: Be true to your own convictions, work for a worthy cause, sacrifice some comfort to accomplish a goal.

There's nothing wrong with basking in successes. Even the Batman — cold, emotionless, driven champion of justice, avenger of evil — has a Trophy Room in his Batcave, filled with reminders of past cases and successes. Driven and single-minded though he is, he too needs to be reminded once in a while of his past successes. It keeps him going. But it's for him alone to enjoy; no one else gets to see it. All that matters is that you be proud of and happy with your work.

Bask in Your Successes

You need your own Trophy Room. Keep a journal of your accomplishments on a daily basis. Record even small successes. Furnish your Trophy Room carefully. Stock it thoughtfully. Walk through it (mentally) periodically.

There will always be some people who do not agree with or even like you no matter how right or how likable you are. Trying to convince everyone that you're right is a waste of time. A person with integrity sometimes does things with which others disagree. That's okay.

You need some way to measure the correctness of your views and behavior, but popular opinion does not always provide a good benchmark. Dig deep inside and listen to the message of your soul. It can usually be trusted.

**What we really need is an inner feeling of honor
which is the only kind of feeling that can really satisfy.
What we spend most of our time looking for is the outer,
illusory kind, which can't nourish us even if we get it. Don't be
fooled pursuing the one when what you need is the other.**

Fame and popularity mean nothing to the Batman. In fact, Bruce Wayne works pretty hard to cultivate that weak, cowardly Bruce Wayne image!

Figure 8-1: Bruce Wayne cultivating a weak, cowardly image.
(Detective Comics #437) © DC Comics

CHAPTER 9

Don't Talk
Too Much

O ne of our greatest gifts is the power of speech. Used correctly, we can improve ourselves and the world around us through language. On the other hand, sharp hurtful words can destroy careers, marriages and friendships. The Torah contains dozens of laws relating to proper speech. One of the themes of these laws is to minimize speech if at all possible. The Talmud advises, "Say little and do much."

What's wrong with talking?

Most talk accomplishes nothing, and distracts you from really doing something. The focus has got to be on doing, on accomplishing, not on talking. All the talk in the world, if not implemented, produces nothing. In fact it can be counterproductive. Talk creates the illusion of productivity and allows us to convince ourselves that we have already done much.

In reality, all the attention we pay to an issue by talking about it usually results in little or no actual progress. This illusion of productivity might just be enough to assuage our conscience that we've already done so much and therefore prevent further—real—work and attention to the problem at hand. (We can be fooled quite easily into believing the craziest things!) Better a single deed than a thousand words.

Excessive talk presents another danger. One of the most powerful resources we humans possess is the faculty of speech. We can use this great gift to inspire, counsel and comfort others. But speech can quickly be robbed of its great power. Too easily, and too often, it is diluted by frivolous, nonsensical talk.

Instead of guarding this precious gift by thinking before we speak and making each utterance valuable, significant and important, many people spend their whole lives talking nonsense. This robs speech of its power. Substantive talk is powerful only if it hasn't been diluted by silly talk.

When a person of few words actually does decide to speak, his words are considered much more seriously than one who loves to hear the

How can you get a handle on this great gift of speech to develop mastery over it? Jewish tradition provides for periods of fasting—not from food, but from words. Try it. Don't talk for five minutes. That's much harder than it sounds at first. Build up slowly from there to, say, seven minutes. If you can do it, you are on your way to being in control of the great power of speech, and in control of yourself.

sound of his own voice. The less a person speaks, the more his words are invested with weight and significance. Words have much more authority and power when they are rare.

Consider this exchange from Detective Comics #707:

The Batman and Robin discover some criminals committing a robbery and promptly wade in to arrest them. One of the crooks sees Robin up close and exclaims, "He's just a kid!"

Figure 9-1 describes Batman's response.

Not a lot of words, to be sure, but you can sense their power. Similarly, an abundance of expressions of gratitude could not communicate what his "Thanks, old friend" does!

> The rule, then, is: If it's not necessary to speak, it's necessary *not* to speak. Instead, keep quiet. Or do something totally radical: listen.

Build up a credit. If you speak only when you have something of substance to share, people will, in time, realize this and will start to consider your words carefully.

Words can never be retrieved. If you had a secret identity, how long would it last? If you had just gone several rounds with the Joker and lived to tell about it, how many minutes would it take before you blabbed to everyone you know?

Figure 9-1: The power of a few well-chosen words. (Detective Comics #707) © DC Comics

CHAPTER 10

The Value
of Idealism

W e live in a world in which people pursue comfort, ease, pleasure and fun. There is a popular bumper sticker that eloquently sums up twenty-first-century Western values when it asks, "If it's not fun, why do it?"

It is interesting to speculate about the Batman's reaction to this bumper sticker, were he to come across it, say, one night while patrolling Gotham City in his Batmobile. Can't you see his eyes narrow, as he spots and reads it? What would he say, through gritted teeth? How much of what he does is fun? How much of what he does is motivated by pursuit of pleasure or comfort or ease?

With a financial empire at his disposal, Bruce Wayne could have chosen to lead an easy, fun life amidst the other Gotham socialites whose values and lifestyle he pretends to share. But if he had, no one would be writing stories about his adventures; and, if anyone did, few of us would read them. Why should we? What would there be to read about? They'd just be stories about soft, pleasure-seeking people like ourselves.

But he chose *not* to pursue pleasure. He chose to dedicate himself to a higher—infinitely higher—value: to fight for justice and to battle evil. To do that, he had to forego all the comfort, ease, pleasure and fun that his billions could have bought him, and with which our society is obsessed. Thank God—for us and for him—that he chose the higher path.

There are ideals worth fighting for that are bigger than our own comfort.

It's darn inconvenient to fight for noble causes. There is not a lot of comfort involved, even less ease, and not much fun at all. Instead, there is discomfort and sacrifice and hard work. By modern society's shallow standards, there is not much payoff in pursuing noble causes.

But what value does life have when it is lived selfishly, without thought or regard for the wellbeing of other people? What is the value of a life

---

Try this exercise, which I picked up from the Duke University Fuqua Business School: Write your own obituary. How will you be remembered? For what values? What will your epitaph say? "Here lies so-and-so, who consumed 10,000 pounds of chicken and 20,000 gallons of soda in his lifetime"? Is that the goal of life?

There is nothing wrong with pleasure or ease or comfort or fun. These are nice additions to life, pleasant perks along the way. Often, they are the rewards for having behaved properly, for having lived a life of value and substance. They are not, and never can be, the end point of our efforts.

lived without idealism? What makes us human? Is it our pursuit of pleasure and fun—or is it our noble, Godly soul?

Figure 10-1 describes how Dick Grayson defines his life, proving that he is a worthy disciple of a worthy mentor.

Here's a funny thing about people: We can't long survive without meaning in our lives, without some moral cause or purpose bigger than ourselves. When people—and society—sink to such low levels that their goal is to have fun, something of their humanity dies. Society begins to unravel. A society that lives for no higher a purpose than the accumula-

Figure 10-1: A life of self-sacrifice is a rich, meaningful life. (Untold Legend of the Batman) © DC Comics

tion of wealth and pursuit of fun cannot long sustain or nourish the human soul that craves meaning and purpose. Look at the malaise that afflicts many young people—and old people, for that matter—in our country. They confront a world devoid of meaning other than accumulation of wealth and pursuit of fun, comfort, ease and luxury, and their souls cry out in pain and wither away.

Choose a goal other than a full belly and a hammock. You'll be amazed at what it can do to invigorate your life. And who knows? Maybe someday we'll be reading about your adventures!

CHAPTER 11

The Value of Strong Principles

How many times have you been exasperated by the sight of the Batman risking his life to save the Joker or some other criminal? "Let him die, Batman! You'll save the world so much trouble later on, when he inevitably escapes in 5 issues!" Why does he bother? Why does he do it?

The Batman has explained many times that it's not for him to decide who should live and who should die. His self-proclaimed goals, among others, include the saving of life. If he subscribes to the notion of the sanctity of human life, then that principle must be obeyed, even when it is annoying or inconvenient, even when his emotions might tell him that it would be great to let this criminal die.

But doesn't Superman also subscribe to this idea? Doesn't he also save the bad guys? Why is this a uniquely Batman value?

Superman does, indeed, save villains' lives, but there is a great, fundamental difference between these two heroes. I don't think it goes against the grain for Superman to pull a crook out of the fire (one which the crook probably caused!) and thus save his life. It seems to me that this kind of behavior is completely consonant with his basic instinct to do Good, and there has never been any great challenge to that altruistic instinct.

Bruce Wayne, in contrast, has suffered greatly from crime and at the hands of criminals. It would be natural, given his rage, if he did not exert himself to save them, if he merely left them to suffer fates they had planned for others.

Who could blame him? But that is the measure of a person's greatness: to keep one's principles even when one's emotions might say otherwise. The Batman's gut might cry out for *revenge*, but he has never wavered from his commitment to *justice*.

This is a tough lesson to learn, and an even tougher one to follow. You

There are many slippery slopes in life, with plenty of opportunities to compromise our principles. If we don't follow our moral principles right down the line, even — especially! — when they are inconvenient, those principles will be eroded beyond recognition and pretty soon we'll be left with nothing other than our own arbitrary whims.

And that's like having no values at all. In fact, it's worse, since we can delude ourselves this way into thinking that we are moral.

Figure 11-1: Dick Grayson swearing an oath to champion justice. (Untold Legend of the Batman) © DC Comics

have to have strong moral values, and you have to follow them even when it is inconvenient. If, for example, you value the sanctity of life only when it is a life that you value, that's a sham; you aren't following that value —you're following your own arbitrary prejudices.

The Batman is well aware of our human capability for moral "corner-cutting" and sloppiness. He is very clear and unequivocal with young Dick Grayson. As Figure 11-1 shows, if Dick wants to become his partner in fighting crime and injustice, there can be no place for moral compromise. An awareness of God's presence and His expectations for us runs through the narrative in the panel. These heroes view their work as nothing less than Divine Service, serving the Almighty by protecting His children. Shouldn't we all have to take this oath?

> *No arsenal, or no weapon in the arsenals of the world, is so formidable as the will and moral courage of free men and women.*
> —Ronald Reagan

There is a power that justice and goodness have. Commit yourself to them fully and you can tap into their inestimable power.

Maintain Your Values and Integrity

I know a community that introduced a simple exercise called "WWBD" to its police department—that is, "What Would Batman Do?"

Sounds stupid? It isn't.

Have you ever had the experience of trying to maintain your position while treading water at the beach? You think you've succeeded…until you notice that the multicolored beach umbrella, which used to be opposite your position on the shore, is now far upshore. While you were chattering away with a friend or contemplating the blue of the sky above, and thinking that you hadn't moved at all, you had drifted far, far away from your original position.

It happens to all of us in our lives.

Constant exposure to emotionally and morally corrosive individuals and situations can cause us to drift from possessing absolute values and standards of morality. Instead of being absolute, they become relative. This can be disastrous—morally, professionally, personally.

How do you maintain a constant, inviolate value system in the face of an onslaught of rationalization, immorality, temptation and situational moral relativity? Isn't it inevitable that the corrosion will change you?

Make a daily position check from the GPS of absolute standards and values of morality. Synchronizing your thoughts and actions against something fixed and unchanging can play the same role as that multicolored umbrella on the beach: You can use it to correct your position and prevent yourself from drifting way downstream toward moral relativism.

"WWBD"—"What Would Batman Do?"—is an exercise that forces you to compare your instincts and behavior to the gold standard of an idealized, perfect, mythical do-gooder. How would the Batman, free from temptation, laziness, callousness, graft and personal self-interest, behave in this situation? How are you behaving in this situation?

Maybe you've floated downstream. Maybe you paddled vigorously to get there. Maybe it's time to correct your position.

"WWBD?" Silly? Perhaps. Light-hearted? Definitely. Stupid? Definitely not.

CHAPTER 12

The Value of Anticipating Consequences

The Batman takes precautions by preparing for upcoming battles with a care and precision that appear at times excessive or worthy of a coward. Not too long ago, as Figure 12-1 relates, Dick Grayson ruefully recalled that, under Batman's tutelage, he was required to learn how to "properly diagnose the symptoms of distinct forms of asphyxiation."

Who would anticipate such a necessity? Is the Batman a control freak or an obsessive-compulsive?

He is none of those things. He is simply wise. Asked to define a "wise" person, the Talmud explains that a wise person is one who anticipates consequences and possibilities down the line.

This is not a natural instinct, but it sure pays off! The natural instinct is to think only of the present and to be concerned only with what our eyes can see and our hands can touch. When the Batman wins, it's because the battle had been fought and won long before the first punch is ever thrown, with all possibilities and contingencies worked out long before. It *has* to be this way: How else could he survive the overwhelming odds against him, one lone man (and a boy) against an army of criminals?

That spectacular, dramatic victory may appear spontaneous and unrehearsed. In fact, it was neither. The Batman's victories are built on forethought, on consideration of the consequences and ramifications of each potential mode of behavior, including the dangers and obstacles that might

Figure 12-1: Dick Grayson gains a new appreciation for Batman's level of preparedness. (Nightwing Annual #1) © DC Comics

Figure 12-2: The importance of considering all the possibilities. (Batman Chronicles: The Gauntlet) © DC Comics

Figure 12-3: Batman anticipates all the possibilities. (Detective Comics #568) © DC Comics

arise. The Batman doesn't leap into the fray before considering all possibilities. And he prepares responses to each and every possible outcome.

Did you ever wonder how Batman manages to have the right equipment in his utility belt every time? The answer, of course, is simple: He's got great writers. (Let's not go overboard here!) But maybe there is another reason as well: his anticipation of the circumstances that he is likely to confront.

For the Batman, to do anything less is foolhardy and irresponsible because lives hang on each and every decision he makes. The stakes probably aren't quite that high for us—but the principle remains the same.

The best solution to a crisis that confronts us is never to have confronted it at all. If we could be prepared at all times for every eventuality, we might, in fact, never encounter any moment of confrontation.

Most of us act with too little regard or thought to possible consequences down the line. We pretend that the future does not exist. Mature minds do not suffer from

Before embarking on a course of action, stop a moment and consider what might be the consequences down the road.

It is better to be prepared for an opportunity and not have one than to have an opportunity and not be prepared.
—Civil rights leader Whitney Young, Jr.

this delusion, and mature people live life in the present with a healthy respect for what the future can bring.

Some forethought now could save a lot of heartache later on down the line. For example, some types of behavior look attractive and gratifying right now, but they carry steep price tags in the future.

This is a tough mental discipline, but it's worth cultivating. Start out slowly and try to anticipate the possible future consequences, five minutes from now, of that choice you are about to make. Try to work your way up to ten minutes—and keep going!

CHAPTER 13

The Value of Study

I n the course of his career, the Batman has drawn on information from chemistry, physics, botany, zoology, ophidia, psychology, literature, forensics, law, medicine, toxicology, religion, mythology, etc. His range of study encompasses other, less savory, topics as well, in accordance with his conviction that "You can't beat crooks until you know their tricks." You would be hard pressed to find an area of study and knowledge that has not come in handy and played a crucial role in one investigation or another.

"Remember, Dick," Bruce Wayne has said repeatedly, "a good education is one thing not even the smartest crook can steal from you."

In the Batman's line of work, each additional piece of information can mean the difference between life and death. Thank God that for most of us the stakes are not that high. But who knows in life what information will be relevant? In fact, all of it is. Each additional bit of knowledge can be used in whatever campaign you engage.

My own experiences as a rabbi have confirmed this truth many times. I am an avid reader and have accumulated a fair amount of broad, if not necessarily deep, information about a wide variety of topics over the years. This has proven invaluable on more than one occasion.

Figure 13-1: Bruce Wayne learning everything he can.
(Untold Legend of the Batman) © *DC Comics*

Many people, both young and old, have an instinctive fear of clergy, and tend to dismiss us as occupied with useless and irrelevant concerns. The knowledge I have gained has allowed me to put them at ease by opening a conversation with a topic which interests them.

Don't dismiss anything as unimportant. Don't forego any opportunity to learn more, about any topic. The opportunity to use your knowledge to advantage will certainly present itself.

Now, perhaps if I can get my wife to agree with this principle, I can convince her to let me keep my collection of books about soil analysis…

CHAPTER 14

The Value
of Friendship

'm not talking about a million superficial, "fair weather" acquaintances. Those aren't *real* friends. I mean a true, close, trustworthy friend.

Rabbi Ben Sira counseled: "Have a thousand acquaintances; but confide only in one true friend." How many of us can say that we have one true friend, in whom we can confide, to whom we can look for help when things are tough? Even more importantly, perhaps, how many of us can say we are such a friend for someone else?

It is impossible to overestimate the value of a true friend. Where would Bruce Wayne / the Batman be without Dick Grayson and Alfred Pennyworth? They have saved his life and his sanity over the years, and he in turn has been there for them.

Don't be fooled by that talk about having no *real* friends in Figure 14-1. The Batman couldn't do what he does without the assistance of his friends. True, Bruce traded in his chance to have a thousand insincere, superficial "friendships." The circle is drawn much smaller. But he gained the potential for something greater: a handful of close, true friends.

Have a thousand acquaintances; but confide only in one true friend.

Figure 14-1: Bruce warning Dick about the loneliness of the job. (Legends of the Dark Knight #100) © DC Comics

*Figure 14-2: The deep level of trust between Batman
and Robin (Tim Drake). (Robin #9) © DC Comics*

True friendship must be earned, however. Bruce Wayne has earned that friendship time and again, day in and day out, not by empty talk, but in real, meaningful ways. He took Dick in and gave him a home; Bruce took Alfred in and gave Alfred's life purpose, a "noble cause."

Friendship doesn't have to be a showy business, with a lot of talking and emoting, to be nourishing. Bruce Wayne, Dick Grayson, Tim Drake, and Alfred Pennyworth don't spend a lot of time discussing their friendship. Such talk would be superfluous and downright absurd. Every one of their

*Figure 14-3: Alfred's deep loyalty
to the Batman and his cause.
(Untold Legend of the Batman)
© DC Comics*

Figure 14-4: The light banter of two
close friends. (Detective Comics #474)
© DC Comics

Figure 14-5: Two friends bid
each other a fond farewell.
(Detective Comics #474)
© DC Comics

actions demonstrates, in ways that mere words could not, the true depth
and extent of their friendship and concern for each other. All the flowery
language of friendship, which amounts to so little, is nothing compared
to the quiet, understated—indeed, unstated—but profound friendship
that these four men, who have been through so much together, share.

Their friendship has grown and matured to resemble a family—the natural result of all true friendship. When you think about it, the Batcave is pretty darn full, with Alfred, Nightwing (Dick Grayson), Robin (Tim Drake), Batgirl/Oracle (Barbara Gordon) and the new Batgirl (Cassandra Cain).

Do you crave true, substantive friendship? Deep friendships are most likely to develop among people who work and sacrifice together for a common goal. Find a worthy cause and throw yourself into it. You'll find that the friendship you seek will be an inevitable, happy byproduct.

> Deep friendships are most likely to develop among people who work and sacrifice together for a common goal.

CHAPTER 15

The Most Effective Way to Fight Evil

W e look up to the Batman, with all that he has accomplished, all the good he has done, in awe. If only we could do what he does, the world would be a much better place!

But whom does the Batman revere and admire? To whom does he look for inspiration? Whose methods does he most admire?

Leslie Thompkins — the woman who never left fashionable Park Row, even after it became the slum called Crime Alley, the idealistic angel of mercy who has spent her life helping its inhabitants. She has waged just as relentless a war against crime and evil with her own arsenal of love, compassion, care, concern and kindness.

The Batman is reactive. He serves as society's last line of defense when its fabric has become frayed at the edges. His job is damage control. As far as that goes, it works.

The Batman's methods are best suited to address the symptoms of societal decay and disintegration. But are they suited to address and reverse the spiritual malaise that lies beneath and spreads like a cancer? No — and he doesn't attempt to address them directly, even though that's really where the true need is.

It is Leslie Thompkins who addresses and directly battles this spiritual malaise. She is *proactive,* and her approach is to stop crime even before it starts by inspiring others to walk the straight and narrow path through her actions. In the long run, her way is the better one.

Stop a criminal career — before it starts.

Plant some seeds for the future. It might require a little effort, but the rewards can be tremendous. You don't need to know what will happen after you plant them.

How many movies involve traveling back through time to change history? What if *you* could travel back through time and dissuade someone from walking that twisted path? Well, guess what? You're back there right now. Do it now.

> "It's easier to build a child than fix an adult."

After witnessing the murder of Thomas and Martha Wayne, Leslie Thompkins dedicated her life to improving the environment in Crime Alley.

*Figure 15-1: Leslie Thompkins dedicated her life to improving
the world. (Detective Comics #457) © DC Comics*

How many of us can do what the Batman does? Not many—perhaps
we have a glass jaw or a bum knee.

But how many of us can do what Leslie Thompkins does? Any one of
us can.

**And, ultimately, who can say whose methods will
produce the greatest, most dramatic, substantive
changes in society? The Batman has eloquently
given us his answer to this question in Figure 15-1.**

CHAPTER 16

The Price
of Greatness

Here's another difficult truth: Real greatness comes at a cost. Something has to give.

Sometimes the cost is reasonably small. I remember reading about an exchange between master musician Fritz Kreisler and a fan. After a concert, he was approached by a woman who exclaimed, "Mr. Kreisler, I would give my life to play as you do!" "Madame," replied the master quietly, "I did."

That's one kind of sacrifice, to be sure. But there are other, more extreme — and sadder — sacrifices.

Bruce Wayne sacrificed his chance for a "normal" life when he decided to spend his life as the Batman. He sacrificed himself in order to ensure that others never have to suffer the tragedy he did.

Jason Todd, the second Robin, made the ultimate sacrifice. He gave his life in the battle against evil. It's the sacrifice the Batman is prepared to make every night of his life.

These are fictional characters, of course. But we encounter greatness in real life, too, and we see the cost of that greatness. When I began to write this book, for example, the news was filled with stories describing the car-

Figure 16-1: Real-life heroes. © NYPost Holdings, Inc.

nage in a high school in Columbine, Colorado. Amidst all that horror and inhumanity is an example of heroism which staggers the imagination. Coach William "Dave" Sanders risked, and ultimately gave, his life to warn students and shepherd them to safety. He made the ultimate sacrifice to ensure the safety of others. How many heroic firefighters, police officers, and rescue personnel chose to run *into* the fiery Twin Towers on 9-11-2001 in order to evacuate the innocent people trapped inside? Their self-sacrificial goodness and heroism is the antidote to the evil to which we are exposed.

Without such episodes to reassure us, how could we ever get out of bed in the morning after seeing the extent of depravity and cruelty of which human beings are all too often capable?

CHAPTER 17
Where Crooks Hide

Crooks always make their hideouts in areas with large deposits of red clay. If you're looking for the bad guys, head straight for that part of the county which has a high concentration of red clay instead of conventional dirt or mud. It's always on the crooks' boots or shoes, and they always leave some at the scene of the crime, in accordance with Locard's Exchange Principle. (Look it up in a criminalistics textbook!) You can check those soil charts and prospecting maps the county government has compiled if you want to, but it's just going to add time to your investigation. It's happened too many times over the years to be a coincidence: Crooks always choose hideouts on the outskirts of town where there's an unusually large concentration of red clay.

Crooks, beware: I have passed this information along to the North Carolina and New Jersey State Police.

Durham, North Carolina, by the way, has an unusually high proportion of red clay. Draw your own conclusions!

*Figure 17-1: The crook's hideout is—surprise!—
in an area with lots of red clay. © DC Comics*

CHAPTER 18

Conclusion

These, then, are the moral Truths I learned, starting at a pretty young age, from reading Batman comic books. These are the ideas that formed the core of what became my philosophy of life. These are the ideas I encountered later in my religious studies. These are the ideas that were later formalized (and deepened and refined, to be sure) in rabbinical school. And these are the ideas I convey in my Torah classes (originally at Duke, the University of North Carolina–Chapel Hill and throughout that state's Research Triangle, and more recently in New Jersey) and in my spirituality presentations at the FBI Academy.

If I am right that these are, in fact, the Truths that define the character of the Batman, then you responded to each of these points with an "Oh, yeah, of course, that's right. I knew that." Do these points seem familiar? As you read and enjoy Batman comic books, do you, too, consciously or otherwise, identify these Truths?

Many, perhaps most, people dream of being heroic. There's nothing wrong with that, of course. It's a fine aspiration.

> **I hope this book serves as a reminder that there are
> countless opportunities around us — opportunities
> that we encounter in our everyday lives — to be heroic.**

They might not require that we scale the sheer face of a mountain, endure arctic weather, possess mastery of a batarang or a black belt in kung fu, or match wits with world-class assassins. But they are no less heroic — that is, if you consider to be a hero someone who helps people and makes a positive difference in their lives, refuses to bow to difficulty or adversity, and possesses integrity and principles in the face of seductive temptation. I sure do.

Every day we dismiss many opportunities — glorious opportunities — to be heroic. We let them slip right past us, never even realize what they are. Do the people we help have to be strangers? Is it any less heroic to help the people around us, perhaps even the members of our own families?

The Batman inspires me. His ideals are ones I personally subscribe to and believe in passionately. Through a lifetime of reading about the Batman I have identified a model for noble behavior — a model which has been refined and confirmed by the teachings of traditional Judaism. My enthusiasm for and receptivity to religious teachings had its origins in a lifelong fascination with the character of the Batman, a fascination that persists to this day.

I'm not alone. I read somewhere that Adam West, the actor who played Batman in the 1960s TV spoof (and now provides the voice of the Gray Ghost in the animated adventure cited above), said that detectives and policemen approach him all the time and tell him that they were inspired by the TV show to choose the careers they did. The TV show had that kind of power, even though it was a campy take-off on the real Batman. Even that kind of a satirical portrayal of the Batman was inspirational! Of course, the Batman whom I met first in the comic books wasn't joking around, like his TV counterpart. He was the driven, grim avenger of the night.

The results of my relationship with the Batman stories are evident in the choices I have made in my life. Because of the Batman, early on in my youth I used some birthday money to buy a set of weights. Because of the Batman, I majored in sciences in college. Most of all, because of the Batman, I entered the rabbinate, with the hope that I could influence others to live more moral, meaningful lives. I have a fear of heights (and an even bigger fear of being beaten up), so emulating the Batman in a literal way was never really an option.

Why, then, did I choose to become a rabbi, of all things? The Hebrew word *"rav,"* from which the English equivalent "rabbi" is derived, is etymologically related to another Hebrew word, *"reev,"* which means "struggle" or "battle." Get it? The idea is that a rabbi is supposed to be a champion on behalf of the Torah and God, against wickedness and for righteousness.

When I made that connection, I sent in my first semester's application fee to rabbinical school right away. The Batman provided me with the idea that struggling and fighting for a noble cause was at the heart of truly heroic behavior. Following Bruce Wayne's lead, I took control of my own life, and made it my goal to commit that life to moral pursuits on the cosmic level.

It's always seemed to me that the people who read Batman tend to be more confident of themselves, of their ability to get the job done and to make a difference in the world than, say, fans of Superman, whose story begins with a gift of enormous, and unearned, power.

Jules Feiffer, in *The Great Comic Book Heroes* (page 27), agrees: "I suspect the Batman school of having healthier egos." Most other heroes gained their powers originally without a lifetime of pain and preparation.

That's not to say that they haven't used them wisely or responsibly once having acquired them.

In sharp contrast, anything Bruce Wayne has attained has been won — or rather, earned — through unstinting hard work. I think that's a large part of the Batman's appeal. If you like the Batman, I think that speaks very highly for you and your confidence in your ability to accomplish in this world.

> **For me, the lesson of the Batman was clear: I stopped waiting around for a radioactive bat to bite me and I started doing sit-ups. It's a policy I've maintained ever since.**

In my own career, I quite often encounter obstacles and difficulties. I come face to face with misfortune and tragedy more often than I'd like to; people in pain find a way to my door. Sometimes the work looks too enormous and overwhelming. Where do I begin? How can I address so much misery? What, after all, can one person do? And, of course, there are always critics and naysayers (all of them jealous of me, my mother assures me) who impugn my motives and best intentions. In fact, while I don't mean to brag or complain, I think it's fair to say that my rogues' gallery makes the Batman's look like a bunch of wimps. (Mine includes a whole army of two-faces, not just one!) Sometimes it appears hopeless.

My natural instinct is to throw up my hands and consider going back to my previous career as a scientist. At those times, thank God, I have a few sources to which I turn for solace and inspiration so that I can return, refreshed and recharged, to my purpose. Traditional Jewish literature is filled with inspirational works which remind me that we are in This World not for our own comfort, but for a larger purpose: to pursue Good and battle Evil. And, of course, the new Batman comic books arrive at the local comic book store on Wednesday morning.

Hi, Pete, Sean, and Chris!

AFTERWORD

I picked a few issues and episodes—some of my personal favorites—to illustrate these lessons, but there are hundreds, perhaps thousands, of other stories that teach the same—and other—lessons.

If you have your own personal favorite stories that illustrate these Truths, or if you can think of other lessons you learned from reading about the Batman, please drop me a line and share your thoughts, ideas, opinions. I'd love to hear from you.

Please write me c/o Compass Books (P.O. Box 3091, Linden, NJ 07036) or at Cary@BatWisdom.com.

ABOUT THE AUTHOR

By day the author is a rabbi in New Jersey and, believe it or not, a consultant to the FBI. He lives in stately Friedman Manor with his wife and children. Despite what he wrote in the introduction, Rabbi Friedman still wears Underoos™.